...And So, We Dance

How to Unlock Intimacy, Passion, and Connection by Dancing in the Kitchen

James and D'Leene DeBoer
Couples Who Dance

First Edition published by Amore Corp. 2022 Copyright

© 2022 by James and D'Leene DeBoer

All rights reserved. This publication is designed to provide accurate and authoritative information regarding the subject matter covered. It is sold with the understanding that neither the authors nor the publisher is engaged in rendering legal, medical, psychological, or other professional services. While the publisher and authors have used their best efforts in preparing this book, they make no representations or warranties with respect to the accuracy or completeness of the contents of this book and specifically disclaim any implied warranties of merchantability or fitness for a particular purpose. No warranty may be created or extended by sales representatives or written sales materials. The advice and strategies contained herein may not be suitable for your situation. You should consult with a professional when appropriate. Neither the publisher nor the authors shall be liable for any loss or damages, including but not limited to special, incidental, consequential, personal, or other damages.

No part of this publication may be reproduced, distributed, or transmitted in any form or by any means, including photocopying, recording, or other electronic or mechanical methods, without the prior written permission of the publisher, except as permitted by U.S. copyright law and fair use. For permission requests, contact admin@coupleswhodance.com with "Permissions" in the subject line.

Designations used by companies to distinguish their products are often claimed as trademarks. All brand names and product names used in this book are trade names, service marks, trademarks and registered trademarks of their respective owners. None of the companies referenced within the book have endorsed the book or given financial incentives.

The authors have no responsibility for the persistence or accuracy of URLs for external or third-party Internet Websites referred to in this publication and does not guarantee that any content on such Websites is, or will remain, accurate or appropriate.

For privacy reasons, some names, locations, and dates may have been changed.

First Edition

Authors: James and D'Leene DeBoer
Cover Design by James and D'Leene DeBoer
Cover Photo by L'Mara Zielinski
Back Cover Photo by Haley Miller Skredsvig
Narration by James and D'Leene DeBoer

979-8-9882229-5-8

TABLE OF CONTENTS

- 07 Acknowledgments
- 15 Dancing Through Life
- 23 The Beginning...And a One
- 31 All You Need Is Love...And Dance!
- 45 The Couples Who Dance Method
- 51 Step 1: Cooperation
- 61 Step 2: Commitment
- 67 Step 3: Connection
- 73 Step 4: Communication
- 81 Let's Dance!
- 87 The Next Dance
- 93 In This Kitchen, We Dance
- 101 Practice, Not Perfection
- 107 Resources

...And So, We Dance

...And So, We Dance

> *"We know it well that none of us acting alone can achieve success."*
>
> *~ Nelson Mandela*

Acknowledgments

To my person,

Writing this book and dancing this life with you is so incredibly humbling, and I'm so grateful. Our book, our retreats, our life, is all borne out of the deep love and partnership we have co-created. Without your unwavering commitment, your patience, your open heart and creative spirit, these pages would remain unwritten. We are breaking through our goals and building our dreams.

Thank you for being my dance partner through all the twists, turns, dips and soaring moments life has brought our way. For choosing to show up fully, even when the music felt distorted. For leading when I needed strength, following when I was in my power, and always meeting me with openness in the sacred dance between our souls. It was your belief in us that gave me the courage to embrace vulnerability

...And So, We Dance

and share our journey so others may find inspiration walking their own path. Your commitment, support, and strength cast the light that guided us through the inevitable storms.

The wisdom contained here was forged in the fires of our experiences, the joys, the growing pains, the simple moments of intimate connection. You remained by my side through it all, steadying my hand, steadying my heart, so that our love story could be written onto these pages. This book is a celebration of the divine partnership we have created together. A toast to the passion that still burns within our bond after all this time. A dedication to our commitment that allows us to choose each other, day after day, without hesitation.

Thank you for being my best friend, for choosing me, choosing Brennan, being my person, my teammate, my forever dance partner through this crazy, beautiful, once in a lifetime life.

Acknowledgments

I love you more,

Wife

***

To my beloved,

I owe immense gratitude to my wife D'Leene. In the dance of life, you have been my perfect partner, guiding with grace and harmony through every step and rhythm. In the grand symphony of life, you are my favorite melody, the rhythm that guides me through each chapter, each verse. Your patience, love, positivity, and unwavering encouragement have been the cornerstone of this journey, lifting me up when doubts cast shadows and celebrating with me in moments of triumph. Every moment spent creating with you is a cherished memory of love and togetherness. Your love is a beacon of light that guides me through life's challenges and triumphs. Your kindness, compassion, and boundless love have shaped me and for that, I am eternally grateful.

...And So, We Dance

You are someone who shows up fully; a positive, kind, empathetic, loving, determined, committed, powerful person. Thank you, my love, for being you.

Adding on to what you said about this book, this book is not just a collection of words; it's a tribute and bares witness to the love, growth, commitment, and journey we've shared and continue to share.

Thank you for being my partner, my confidante, and my best friend. May our love continue to dance through the melodies of life, forever intertwined in the beautiful tapestry of our shared dreams.

With all my love,

James

Acknowledgments

***

To our amazing son, Brennan,

You are such an incredible young man and have our whole hearts. You are the beautiful culmination of the passion that burns within the bond we have created together after all this time. We are thankful everyday we get to watch you grow up and to be your parents.

Just as this book is a celebration of the partnership we have built, and you are the living embodiment of that partnership. The wisdom gained through our joys, growing pains, and intimate moments as parents was forged in the fires of experience. The ups and downs of being a blended family has only strengthened the bond we have. Your dad chose to be your dad and chooses in every day, not out of obligation by blood and instead by the power of love and commitment. All along, your mother remained steady, loving, and optimistic so our family's love story could be written onto these pages of life.

...And So, We Dance

Brennan, you are our cherished melody, the rhythm that guides us through each new chapter and verse of this crazy, beautiful journey. Your mother's kindness, compassion and boundless love have shaped you, and for that we are eternally grateful. May the dreams we've built together continue to dance through the melodies of our family's life, forever intertwined.

You are a reminder to choose each other day after day, without hesitation. We love you with every fiber of our beings and look forward to watching you create your dreams and the choreography for your life. You have an incredible heart, so much love and wisdom, your kindness and inclusivity are inspiring, and we are proud to be your parents. Keep Being you and we love you more!

With eternal love,

Mom and Dad

...And So, We Dance

> *"In the arms of a dance partner, I found a connection deeper than words could convey. Each step became a dialogue, an unspoken exchange of emotions that transcended the boundaries of conversation."*
>
> *~ D'Leene DeBoer*

Dancing Through Life

D'Leene's Dance Journey:

I never truly understood the profound impact dance could have on my life until I found myself navigating the challenging waters of loss and trauma. Life had thrown its toughest punches, leaving me in a state of emotional disarray. In those moments of despair, I stumbled upon an unexpected lifeline, the art of dance.

How do you tell a wounded soul to find solace in rhythmic movements and twirls? How could the simple act of dancing become a beacon of hope in the darkest corners of my existence? I didn't have the answers then, but I knew I needed something more than mere survival; I needed a source of joy, connection, and healing. Little did I realize that dance would become the key to unlocking a thriving relationship with passion, intimacy, and profound human connection.

As the first hesitant steps found their way onto the dance floor, I discovered a world where words were unnecessary. The language of the body, expressed through every graceful sway and synchronized step, spoke volumes that my heart could comprehend. In the embrace of the music, I learned to listen not just with my ears but with the core of my being. The rhythms became a heartbeat, syncing with my own, creating a therapeutic symphony that drowned out the noise of my troubles.

In the arms of a dance partner, I found a connection deeper than words could convey. Each step became a dialogue, an unspoken exchange of emotions that transcended the boundaries of conversation. I discovered the power of vulnerability, as the dance floor became a sacred space where masks fell away, and authenticity took center stage. There was an intimacy in those moments, a shared vulnerability that forged connections stronger than any I had experienced before.

I danced through the pain, twirled through the tears, and pushed through the uncertainties. The dance floor became my canvas, and the movements were strokes of resilience painting the masterpiece of my personal transformation. I learned that passion was not just reserved for the grand stages; it could be found in the simple joy of moving in harmony with another human being.

Through dance, I learned that a thriving relationship with passion, intimacy, and connection is not a luxury but a necessity for the soul. It's a reminder that life's hardships can be faced with grace, and healing is not a destination but a continuous journey. The dance floor became my sanctuary, a place where I could celebrate the resilience of the human spirit and express gratitude for the simple joy of being alive.

...And So, We Dance

As I twirled away the pain and embraced the rhythm of life, I realized that dance was not just a set of steps; it was a metaphor for the journey we all undertake. We stumble, we fall, and in the dance of life, we rise again, transformed, and stronger. So, to anyone grappling with the shadows of their own struggles, I say, let the music guide you, let the dance be your refuge, and discover the transformative power of passion, intimacy, and connection. For in the dance, we find not only rhythm but also the resilience to navigate the intricacies of life's ever-unfolding choreography.

***

James's Dance Journey:

Through my day-to-day life I was looking for something to do that was fun, that would challenge me and that I could do with friends. Most of my time revolved around working and activities with close friends such as hiking, biking, rock climbing, going to the gym, gaming, and social evenings at bars.

Another thing I spent time on was going out on dates in an attempt at finding that special someone. On one of those dates, it was proposed to go out dancing; something I had been very nervous about and had never tried before except in middle school where they made us learn the waltz box-step. Nevertheless, I said yes, this was the first step to a whole new world.

What I have experienced in dance has been a warm friendly community full of intelligent incredible people, new friends, new experiences, and getting to connect in a way with others I have not before. To summarize into single words, Community, Connection, and Love. Dance is where I have found lifelong friends, community, unforgettable memories, constant growth, challenge, fun, and my life partner.

...And So, We Dance

Keep in mind, I lean on the side of being an introvert. What I found in dance is how words are not needed, a conversation can happen through your movement and connection with your partner. And to truly connect just like how you are to have a conversation, both need to have a foundational understanding of the language. Both need to be open to listening to each other and tossing the conversation back and forth between one another. A constant one-sided conversation can become boring to be in and to hear.

This conversation through dance is different for every person, as it should be. Every person might hear and feel something different in the music or have a different interpretation. The music itself can have a different tempo, rhythm, energy, and style. This is where the fun challenge comes in where we connect with one another and bring out creativity without compromising the partnership and this one of kind conversation you get to have with this other person.

Dancing Through Life

Has every conversation you have ever had been great? Not for me, I have experienced misunderstandings, interruptions, weird or awkwardness, you name it. The same goes for dancing, not every dance you have with someone is going to be amazing. Be aware one of the easiest things we can do is to be hard or unkind to ourselves which will eventually bleed onto those who are close to us. We cannot expect ourselves to have a perfect conversation every time with every person, this will set ourselves up to be disappointed. Expectation is premeditated disappointment so don't set yourself or a partner up for failure. We have to get through messy to get to clean and we have to get through awkward to get to great.

...And So, We Dance

> *"Love isn't always easy, it's not perfect or linear. Love is overcoming obstacles and choosing in every moment, every day. Facing challenges together and knowing you accomplished something together that would have been impossible without the other."*
>
> *~ D'Leene DeBoer*

The Beginning...And a One

When we were younger, we were socially conditioned to believe that once you find "the one", everything would be blissful, a constant state of harmony, intense passion, deep connection, and effortless intimacy. We would be blessed with unicorns and puppies galore! Well, as D'Leene's psychology professor says "life, life's", and it taught us some tough lessons about how that's not quite reality.

We used to think that arguments or disagreements with your partner were red flags that the relationship was doomed. People often point to conflicts as "evidence" that the relationship was never meant to be, as a way to avoid taking responsibility. We humans have a habit of finding ways to absolve ourselves, a survival mechanism that can

...And So, We Dance

unfortunately undermine love, connection, intimacy, and happiness in our closest relationships, especially marriage.

The truth is, even when you've found your soulmate, the "right" person for you, the learning, growing, and navigating challenges together never stops. You decide if you choose grace and love, especially in the moments when one or both of you aren't being very lovable on the surface. We've been on a journey to continually deepen our love, intimacy, and connection from the beginning, because we've witnessed first-hand what happens when couples get complacent. That's why we want to share what has worked for strengthening the passionate, connected, intimate relationship of our dreams - to empower other couples to do the same. It is possible, even when it feels impossible.

Our journey and story started nearly at the same time. D'Leene and James were both reluctant to going out and dancing, finally D'Leenes friends were able to get her out and James was invited by a girl he could not say no to. It was a local dance

The Beginning...And a One

event that D'Leene and James first met, James instantly knew she was something extremely different, something extra special. At the time, she was married to someone else, so James resigned himself to being only friends. Neither of them could have predicted that just a year later, D'Leene's then-husband would issue an ultimatum, accept his controlling ways or he would seek a divorce. D'Leene loved herself too much to say yes to that and made the difficult choice to leave.

A big part of the ultimatum was that she could no longer dance, it was definitely something her husband wasn't interested in that empowered and lifted D'Leene's spirit. Looking back, it reflected a lack of growth mindset and selfishness that had spilled into other areas of the marriage. James was there to listen as D'Leene tried to save the relationship, and ultimately, she decided that separating was the healthiest path for her and her son.

While D'Leene picked up the pieces, James patiently waited, knowing the kind of incredible woman he

...And So, We Dance

wanted and that she was it. He dated, and never rushed into anything, learning about himself until he felt ready. When D'Leene made the decision to move on, James took his shot, telling her: "I've thought about everything. I love you. I've loved you since I met you, and I just accepted you were happily married and it would never happen between us, but I've been looking for someone like you. As far as Brennan's concerned, he's mine, I don't want him to think he is loved any differently. With the infertility it doesn't matter, I just want you."

D'Leene was blown away that he accepted her son as his own and understood what mattered most to her. She knew he meant it. So, she agreed to move slowly and see if a real future could blossom between them, and they could move forward from there.

At first, D'Leene's subconscious fears had her put up walls, showing James the worst version of herself in an attempt to push him away because she would rather do it all alone than have someone who would leave. James never gave up because he knew her well, proving his commitment day after day until those walls came down. Friendship blossomed into an unbreakable partnership.

We've walked through fire, rain, and hail together - the ups and downs of blending families, legal battles, deaths of loved ones, careers, entrepreneurship, and all the other challenges adulthood throws your way. As D'Leene said in her vows: "Love isn't always easy, it's not perfect or linear. Love is overcoming obstacles and choosing in every moment, every day. Facing challenges together and knowing you accomplished something together that would have been impossible without the other."
...and so, we dance.

Through the fire, the rain, the hail, through it all, we dance. In our kitchen, throughout the US, on beaches in Maui, streets of Canada, Paris, Germany, and Ireland, everywhere we are, we dance. Dance is where we come together, connect, feel each other's hearts and souls. It's about being utterly present with your partner and the music moving through you both. Surrendering with our person to vulnerability and intimacy in a way that is unmatched.

...And So, We Dance

As the author Amelia Atwater-Rhodes said: "In a society that worships love, freedom and beauty, dance is sacred. It is a prayer for the future, a remembrance of the past and a joyful exclamation of thanks for the present." In difficult moments, dance grounds us and reminds us why we chose to do this journey together. It's like the advice for couples to hold hands when they argue, magnified tenfold. When you melt into each other's arms and move as one, you remember this is your person, your teammate with you in the trenches. We don't get to choose the music life plays for us, but we get to choose who we dance with to it.

Our vision is for every couple to discover the profound intimacy, connection, and passion that dance can inspire in their own relationship, just as it has in ours. We know our experience isn't unique, and we hope our story resonates with you as you embark on that exploration together. So put on a record, hold your love close, and start dancing through this crazy life as an inseparable, seamless partnership.

The Beginning...And a One

Come dance with us!

...And So, We Dance

> *"Dance is your pulse, your heartbeat, your breathing. It's the rhythm of your life. It's the expression in time and movement, in happiness, joy, sadness and envy."*
>
> *~ Jacques d'Amboise*

All You Need Is Love...And Dance!

Dance is the non-verbal embodiment of communication, connection, and intimacy; it allows couples to go to depths with each other they didn't know existed. Dance is a key to the 4 main steps (pun intended) we see in strong marriages which we cover in the next section.

Dance is the place where we feel completely free from the mental, emotional, and physical stresses of life. Where we are fully immersed in each other, the music, and the movements together. There are many reasons dance holds this space for many. Music is as primal for us as movement. We even have music therapy to treat a wide range of issues for people. Dance is the act of movement to music intensifying the therapeutic effects of music. When you merge that with dancing with the person you love, the earth moves. It's the best way to reset, reconnect and move forward in love with your partner. This has been our way to keep that spark in our love alive.

Intimacy is key, and it often gets distorted to mean sex or sexual contact. This confusion of intimacy is more common among men and younger individuals, especially in the United States. An example is believing that a romantic dinner or sexual activity is expressing intimacy or genuine vulnerability. This is most often the way men think about intimacy and often why they reach to sexual activity in an attempt to feel intimacy. Sex doesn't require intimacy and can often be a barrier to true intimacy leaving people feeling this emptiness and longing for connection.

Love, sex, and intimacy are not interchangeable. They can all coincide with one another or be independent of the other. We might be jumping into a controversial arena here, but you can have sex without love, intimacy, authenticity, or vulnerability. You can love and have intimacy without a thread of sex or sexual energy. However, you can have deeper love, better sex, and connection when intimacy is present. Let's breakdown love, sex, and intimacy, so we are all on the same page and speaking the same language. Then we will explain how dance affects intimacy in powerful ways. To ensure we are all on the same page when using terms, we want to give some detail on some that have confusion on their meaning. We will explain them as we introduce them below.

Love is a complex and multifaceted emotion that encompasses a broad spectrum of feelings, actions, and connections. It goes beyond mere affection and is often described as a profound sense of attachment, care, and understanding. Love can manifest in various forms or levels, including romantic love, platonic love, familial love, and even self-love. It involves a deep emotional bond, mutual respect, and a willingness to support and nurture the well-being of others. Love is often characterized by acts of kindness, empathy, and selflessness. It has the power to bring joy, fulfillment, and a sense of purpose to individuals' lives. Love is a force that surpasses boundaries, fosters meaningful relationships, and plays a central role in the human experience, influencing our actions, decisions, and the overall quality of our connections with others. A clear

...And So, We Dance

example of this is polyamory. It is the act of having many deeply loving relationships with others and is not tied to, nor does it always include sexual activity. Where polysexuality doesn't require or always include love. We use these examples because people confuse polyamory with polysexual relationships just like they do intimacy with sex or sexual activity. These are separate and understanding the difference is vital to elevating your relationship.

Sex is a fundamental aspect of the human experience and is a diverse and complex expression of physical connection. It can go beyond the biological act, encompassing a range of emotions, desires, and shared moments between individuals. It can also be detached from the emotional intricacies often associated with love and intimacy. Sex can remain neutral, focusing on the physicality of the experience rather than delving into the emotional or relational aspects. In general, this can help explain why some can maintain polysexual relationships without temptation away from their primary partner with whom they share love and intimacy.

Intimacy is intricately woven into the fabric of human connection. It surpasses the physical to become an intense expression of spiritual closeness, being fully seen, and mutual recognition of your human vulnerability. It involves a deep emotional connection, a shared vulnerability, and a mutual understanding that binds individuals together. The transformative power of intimate connections, and the shared vulnerability, fosters growth and understanding between individuals that is unparalleled. Many best friends share a deeply intimate connection as it is a proven safe space for vulnerability and being fully accepted as an imperfect human.

When sex is merged with love and intimacy, it is not merely a transaction of physical pleasure but a dance, an intimate language spoken through the body. It mirrors the emotional symphony between individuals, a moment where desires, trust, and mutual understanding converge. It's a shared vulnerability and understanding that goes beyond the surface. Like skilled dancers moving in synchronized rhythm, the physical act of sex becomes a canvas upon which love paints its vibrant hues, and intimacy weaves the delicate threads of emotional connection. This dance is not a mere

...And So, We Dance

sequence of steps but a heartfelt choreography that transforms the participants, forging a bond that goes beyond the boundaries of the physical realm. It is in the interweaving of these elements that individuals discover a holistic and deeply enriching experience, where passion meets emotion, and vulnerability becomes the foundation for deep human connection.

Dance, with its connected movements and rhythmic expressions, serves as a unique and powerful catalyst for enhancing intimacy between individuals. As partners navigate the dance floor, the physical closeness and synchronized steps create a shared language that transcends words. The art of dance demands a heightened level of communication, fostering a deep connection, trust, and mutual understanding between partners. The act of moving together, whether in the stretched connection of west coast swing or the hypnotic movements of blues, dance encourages vulnerability and trust. In the embrace of the dance, barriers dissolve, allowing an intimate exchange of emotions that words often struggle to convey. It is through the subtle cues, the gentle touch, and the shared energy on the dance floor that a deeply felt sense of closeness is nurtured, enhancing not only the physical connection but also the emotional intimacy between dancers.

All You Need Is Love...And Dance!

Dance becomes a sacred space where partners can authentically express themselves, forging a bond that extends beyond the dance floor into the intricacies of their relationship.

As you can see love, sex, and intimacy are not interchangeable. The problem is we get confused and mix these things together. When someone touches us or holds our gaze for a long time, our primal brain connects it to sex. This is a fun fact about our primal brain that often gets us into trouble, when we used to stare longer than three seconds, we either wanted to eat it or have sex with it. Our brains have not stopped receiving information in some of these primal ways, so we get uncomfortable with staring, especially directly into the eyes. The more you know!

A male friend of ours highlighted that when the pandemic hit, and he no longer had dancing with others, he realized that outside of dance he was rarely ever touched or shown affection. Dancers are more comfortable showing affection and sharing touch than non-dancers. We learn the separation from sex. During this time there was an interview with a trans man who noted the difference in physical and emotional connection he experienced. Living as a woman there was an abundance and living as a male the only time, he experiences this is with family or sexual partners. Untangling these definitions is key to the future health of men and women in our society.

Dance forces us to draw distinctions between love, sex, and intimacy. Unless you fall in love and/or have sex with everyone you dance with, your brain needs to reconcile how to express the physical and emotional vulnerability. Dancing with another person is intimate because it's vulnerable. It's a full body, contact sport, that involves touching, being touched, creative expression and creative vulnerability, as well as moving in a way that's almost codependent. What your body does affects the other person in tangible ways that are physical, visceral, and emotional. It's profoundly beautiful, exciting, and terrifying all at the same time. Because our society has largely blurred the lines between intimacy and sex, we don't know how to navigate the differences. This means we are still learning how to express intimacy and venerability without attaching it to sex. There are some who know the difference and may not have honest intentions which is why clear boundaries that are respected are vital.

Vulnerability and intimacy are everywhere in partner dancing. It's in asking another to dance, dancing late night in a west coast swing ballroom, dancing in a small bar to live music, blues dancing at 2am on a dance cruise, practicing and refining technique with your partner. Learning dance is learning a non-verbal language with depth and meaning in every movement, especially the small ones. This enhances our self-awareness in wonderful ways, so we can show up more fully and present in our authenticity. Watching others dance is getting a glimpse into their true selves, their pure heart, their soul set free in expression. Getting to experience that, dancing with the person you love most, is such a beautiful gift and privilege we want for everyone.

"To watch us dance is to see our souls speak."

~ James and D'Leene DeBoer

...And So, We Dance

Creative vulnerability, well, this came from our amazing friend and coach Joshua Ludlum. He shared drawing art he had produced, he is also a dancer, so when he said that sharing his drawing art felt like "creative vulnerability" dancing immediately came to mind. It is this very vulnerability that allows intimacy to flourish. This intimacy doesn't just apply to our partner, it is with ourselves as well. The feeling of connecting with another person, the music and the dance floor is an unleashing of our spirit. After you have experienced this release of your soul to be truly free it is easier to access it in other areas of your life. It opens so many opportunities in your relationship and life in a very powerful way.

Dance can be a safe space, where we all feel this raw, open, naked, vulnerability. As such we aren't in judgment of others, only ourselves, and it's through learning how to not judge ourselves we stop judging others in our lives, especially our partner. It's a reminder that you're in this together, you need each other to get through this and grow stronger. You are

All You Need Is Love...And Dance!

trusting each other to hold space for all the parts of yourselves, to influence, direct, redirect, create, make creative variations, and most powerfully, their soul. For someone to say "yes" to sharing all of this with you is a gift and privilege. Taking care of them in this experience also means taking care of yourself because both need nurturing. Dance instructors hold a huge impact on this as many grew up being "trained" to dance in a professional and/or competitive manner and they don't think about those of us who simply do this because it's a fun way to connect, have physical activity, etc. Talk to the teacher about your goals and if their teaching style doesn't put you at ease then see what other teachers are around. We aren't all the same and it doesn't mean anyone is wrong here. You should feel safe, welcomed, and encouraged.

In the intimacy of dance, no verbal words are needed. Dance doesn't need backstory, explanations, insight into personal life, relationships, gender, sexuality, race, religion, education, economic status, etc. You are sharing an experience where you get to be known at a soul level. This is a surrender of part of ourselves to this partnership in order to create something together that is bigger and more beautiful than we could ever create on our own. This is what

...And So, We Dance

makes dancing with our partner so powerfully intimate, passionate, and rewarding.

Can you dance without intimacy, kind of. It doesn't require intimacy, feeling vulnerable or connecting authentically. It requires skills, athleticism, and music awareness. However, to create dance artistry, well, it takes intimacy to create a masterpiece. You cannot BS true art because true art comes from the heart, and the heart is fully expressed through intimacy. Your relationship with your partner cannot be BS either and is fully experienced when intimacy is at the center. Dance is a great way to get there faster, with more fun and passionate play together.

All You Need Is Love...And Dance!

...And So, We Dance

> *"Dance is a language beyond words, expressing that for which we have no words."*
>
> *~ Jennifer De Leon*

The Couples Who Dance Framework

When in doubt, dance it out. The rhythmic motions of dance provide the perfect metaphor for gliding together through the swings (*pun intended and endorsed*) of life. Just as in dance partners intertwine in synchronized harmony, couples can use the foundational steps and connections of dance to have seamless cooperation, unwavering commitment, profound connection, and intuitive, flowing, communication within their relationship. This embodied practice serves as our framework for building the lasting intimacy and passion that goes beyond the dance floor, reverberates through every aspect of their lives together, and remains long after the music stops playing. By consciously following the 4 steps, couples can choreograph a partnership rooted in purpose and meaning. So, embrace your person, tune into the rhythm between you, and allow the music to

...And So, We Dance

guide you in this beautiful dance called life, trusting in each other every step of the way.

We will break down each of the steps in a brief overview here and then in more detail in the following chapters.

There are 4 basic steps:

- **Step 1 - Cooperation:** Lead/Follow

- **Step 2 - Commitment:** Partnering

- **Step 3 - Connection:** Creating Together

- **Step 4 - Communication:** The Dance of Life

The first step is cooperation - This is the foundation upon which the dance in partnership builds. Lead/follow is freestyle and allows you to create as the music of life changes where choreography is the pre-decided movements/goals for your shared vision in life. Being responsible, speaking honestly, accepting each other's perspectives with an open mind, offering consistent support, and aligning on your shared vision. To lead and follow means being open to each other's ideas, taking turns leading and following, giving, and receiving in the conversation in the dance just as is needed in life. Cooperation allows you to lead and follow in fluid reciprocity with care, grace, and attunement, while nurturing the spark of intimacy and passion that drew you together.

The second step is commitment - Commitment is the core driving force propelling you forward through the intricate choreography ahead, wholeheartedly choosing this partnership, leaning in with presence and empathy every single moment. Honor truths and agreements that elevate your bond. Uplift and champion each other's strengths to set yourselves up for success in unity. When life's challenges arise, and the music is difficult, you both commit to moving through it all together with love, patience, and rhythm.

...And So, We Dance

The third step is connection - The connection in the dance of life deepens through expressions of love, belonging and vulnerability. Surround yourselves with supportive communities aligned with your values for encouragement and inspiration. Allowing vulnerability is a key to better connection and creating together. Just as the songs change so do the dances and every dance is a new conversation. Tune into the palpable spiritual and energetic frequency between you through practices like dance that unite your creative energies as one.

The fourth step is communication - Through the eloquent nonverbal language of dance you can intuit each other's thoughts, feelings and needs with exquisite clarity. Interpreting the physical, verbal, and energetic signals intuitively as you flow in harmony together allows you to synchronize in the dance of life. Accepting missteps gracefully as opportunities to reinforce your unity to build trust and attunement in your partnership. When you are fully immersed in this passionate dance of life together, your relationship becomes a living work of art that only the two of you can create together.

The Couples Who Dance Framework

These 4 steps have been really great for us and our relationship to simplify staying on the timing for our dance in life together, or getting back on time when we are off for whatever comes up that throws us off. We aren't perfect and that's never the point. It's how we adjust to the music of life and dance forward together through lead/follow getting back to the choreography we decided for the dance of our life together.

As you incorporate these 4 fundamental steps of cooperation, commitment, connection, and communication into your shared dance/life practice, your dance partnership provides a powerful metaphor and methodology to cultivate the thriving intimacy, passion and purpose that allows your partnership to stand the test of time. So, hold your person close, feel their heart beating against yours, and sway fearlessly into the unknown with unbridled trust as you dance this delicate yet resilient dance of life as one.

...And So, We Dance

> *"When someone is the song to your heart's rhythm, dance with them through the swings of life."*
>
> *~ James and D'Leene DeBoer*

Step 1 - Cooperation: Lead/Follow

Cooperation is the foundation of a harmonious partnership. Just as dancers rely on cooperation to move seamlessly in sync, couples require a foundation of deep cooperation to truly thrive in the dance of life. This cooperation is the fertile soil from which all other aspects of a passionate long-term partnership can blossom and grow resilient over time.

On the dance floor, cooperation begins with both partners taking full responsibility for their respective roles and being radically honest about their physical, mental, and emotional availability in any given moment. Each partner comes to the dance floor with 100% responsibility for themselves. Two, whole, responsible individuals coming together to create a future. It requires letting go of any tendency

...And So, We Dance

to cast blame, shame, or judgment when missteps occur. Instead, approach each other with open acceptance, honoring the fact that you each have equally valid yet potentially differing perspectives on situations that arise. In fact, it is these differing perspectives that you can champion to create success. Think of any missteps as a creative variation rather than a mistake.

Maintain this presence of neutral, non-judgmental understanding by releasing any need to be "right" and avoiding the human pitfall of manufacturing problems where none exists. Support one another by assuming good intentions lie underneath even the most charged disagreements or externa conflicts. Rarely is the discord between you actually about you as individuals. More often, it simply stems from the great complexity of two impassioned souls doing their utmost to walk the same path together while still honoring your individuality. Remember you're a team and in this together.

Acknowledging each other's experience and apologizing for any hurt, unintentional or not, is

Step 1 - Cooperation: Lead/Follow

vital to reconciling any conflict so you can move forward and not bring it with you. When you listen and stay curious about how your partner feels and see it from their perspective you can let them know you can see why they might feel or see it that way. You do not need to agree or understand it to accept and acknowledge their perspective or feelings. The simple act of saying something like "thank you for sharing and I'm sorry I hurt you. That wasn't my intention, and I can see how you would feel that way" can immediately diffuse any tension in a misunderstanding. Coming from this place transforms whatever the disagreement or misunderstanding is from you being against each other to being in a team together. It helps the other person feel seen, heard, and cared about. Not doing this can be like adding gun powder to the fire creating a bigger gap to overcome. No one is "right", "wrong" or to blame, so focus on how to create resolution through seeing each other fully.

When you meet inevitable challenges from this open, neutral space of acceptance and acknowledgement, you create the inner foundation required for nurturing incredible intimacy on all levels, intellectual, emotional, experiential, mental, as well as through both verbal and nonverbal channels of

...And So, We Dance

communication. Picture Clydesdale horses. They can pull upwards of eight thousand pounds individually; as a pair they can pull over twenty-four thousand pounds. However, a pair trained together, working in harmonious cooperation can pull weights of thirty-two thousand pounds or more. You and your partner can access unworldly strength and resilience by choosing to be each other's dedicated teammate.

To illuminate the way, focus on cultivating a crystal-clear shared vision of your core values, goals, and life purposes. These overarching intentions bind you together through any storm, serving as guiding lights that empower you to navigate inevitable obstacles as a united front rather than as adversaries. As the amazing Alison Armstrong shares from her research on our primal brains, women tend to have a more diffuse peripheral awareness while men can intensely focus, celebrating these differing superpowers allows you to leverage the best of both in your cooperative partnership.

For true cooperation is not about rigid role adherence or taking turns leading and following. It

Step 1 - Cooperation: Lead/Follow

is an intricate dance of exchanging the baton gracefully, depending on which of you has the most appropriate acuity for any given situation. A mutual surrender into the sense of belonging and being in this together, eagerly embracing the opportunity to shine in a supportive role when your partner's talents best serve your greater good in that moment.

Most importantly, no matter what arises between you, make the conscious choice to nurture intimacy at every available opportunity. Whether through intellectual discourse expanding your perspectives, emotional exchanges that bare vulnerabilities, adventures creating shared meaning, or even mundane moments where you choose to truly see each other's imperfect humanity with fresh eyes. When intimacy is actively nurtured, you lay the groundwork for a depth of connection that flows like a mighty river beneath everything, carrying you through life's turbulent rapids while replenishing your bond with revitalizing perspective, if you allow it.

...And So, We Dance

In those moments when coming together feels impossible, do not stay in it and fight each other. Separate with love, understanding and neutrality. Agree to come back together at a specified time, and resist judging the situation, your partner's perspective, or your partner's journey. Create the required space for each person to realign with their deepest truths in their own way and at their own pace, holding yourselves and each other in unconditional acceptance, devoid of shame or agenda. Remember, each of you holds 100% responsibility only for your own emotional experience, not your partner's. When you both come to the dance floor, being responsible for yourself and acknowledging the part you play in a given situation; it removes the ability to blame, or for your partner to feel they need to defend themselves. This allows both people to feel seen and heard so you can look at what doesn't align with your shared vision or goals and move forward together with what does.

Approach each reunion not as opponents hastily trying to resolve a problem, but as caring friends working alongside each other in service of upholding the highest vision for each other and your relationship. Let go of any need to be "right", and ask in humble curiosity "What is the most

Step 1 - Cooperation: Lead/Follow

responsible, honest, and supportive way for us to move forward together in a way that nurtures our bond, our hopes for this partnership, our shared vision, and goals, and the intimacy we both crave?" Come from an open heart, compassion, and unwavering empathy for the human on the other side of the ring who has bravely committed to walking this path towards the future by your side. This is true cooperation in harmony with your person.

Cooperation is multi-layered. Being 100% responsible, having acceptance, honesty, consistent support, empathy, compassion, and shared purpose will allow you to create the kind of synergistic, unified force that is exponentially greater than either of you could create alone. Just as dancers united in technical precision and authentic presence create lingering imprints of awe in all who bear witness. So do couples adhering to these cooperative fundamentals become living works of art as inspirations for what is possible when two beings decide to truly show up and bring out the highest potential in one another through this wild dance called life. Within such sweet cooperation, you provide the safe shelter required for your love to expand into its most radiant fullest expression, one that illuminates the world and reminds all who

...And So, We Dance

experience your bond that we are ALL meant to live, love, and dance this existence in joyous harmony with our person.

...And So, We Dance

> *"Love is a decision, it is a judgment, it is a promise. If love were only a feeling, there would be no basis for the promise to love each other forever. A feeling comes and it may go. How can I judge that it will stay forever, when my act does not involve judgment and decision."*
>
> *~ Erich Fromm*

Step 2 - Commitment: Partnering

In the world of partner dancing, commitment allows magic to happen. Just as dancers commit fully to their partner, the music, the dance, and any difficult choreography they encounter, couples must learn to embrace commitment in their relationships to create something truly beautiful and enduring.

Think of when dancers practice their choreography leading up to a huge show. They decide before creating together that nothing will get in the way of them executing this dance together. They practice through any pain, illness, or other struggles that come their way. The night of the show they come together and stand behind the curtain ready to give it everything they have for the audience and more so for each other. If at any point either of them gives up or doesn't show up, no matter the reason, it

...And So, We Dance

breaks trust and makes continuing to practice or perform that much harder. Our commitment to our partnership in the dance of life is no different and the stakes are even higher. When you step onto the dance floor, you make a choice to surrender to the moment, to trust your partner, and to give yourself fully to the experience. You lean into each movement, each beat of the music, without hesitation, and give it your all. This is the essence of commitment, embracing the choice and intention to be present, engaged, and connected with your partner, no matter what challenges the dance may bring.

As you move together, you tune into the unspoken language of your partnership, the subtle cues and signals that guide your steps. You listen deeply, not just with your ears but with your heart, feeling the rhythm of your partner's soul. This is the dance of commitment in relationships. Moving together with empathy, awareness, and acceptance, making conscious choices that honor the sacredness of your bond, your vision and partnership.

Step 2 - Commitment: Partnering

In dance, as in love, there will be moments when the choreography gets tough; when the steps seem impossible to master. It's in these moments that your commitment shines through. You don't give up or step out of the dance. Instead, you choose to lean in, to support each other, and to keep moving forward, one step at a time. Setting each other up for success is crucial in this dance of commitment. You identify each other's strengths, provide feedback from a place of love, and celebrate the victories, big and small. You learn from the missteps, the missed connections, and the off-beat moments, knowing that growth and resilience lie on the other side of adversity.

There may be times when the allure of a new dance, a new partner, or a new style may tempt you to stray from your path. In those moments, you anchor yourself in the depth of your commitment, remembering the beauty and magic of the dance only you can create together. When conflicts arise, when the rhythm of your relationship feels off-kilter, choose to dance in the rain. Move through the challenges with patience, grace, and a determination to weather the storm as a united front. Lean into the discomfort, trusting that your commitment to each other will guide you through.

...And So, We Dance

Just as commitment in dance is not about perfection and instead, is about showing up fully, committed relationships are about the willingness to be present, imperfectly, day after day. It's about 100% responsibility for your own emotions, actions, and choices while extending compassion and understanding to your partner. As you continue to dance through life together, your commitment will be tested, just as it is on the dance floor. With each challenge you overcome, each new step you master, your bond will grow stronger, your love will deepen, and your dance will grow as a work of art.

In the end, commitment in relationships, like commitment in dance, is a daily choice. It's the decision to keep showing up, to keep leaning in, and to keep dancing, no matter what the music of life plays. And in that unwavering commitment, you'll find the freedom to love more deeply, live more fully, and dance more joyously than you ever thought possible. So, take your partner's hand, step onto the dance floor of life, and embrace the beautiful, messy, and awe-inspiring journey of commitment. Your greatest dance awaits.

...And So, We Dance

> *"Dance becomes a sacred space where partners can authentically express themselves, forging a bond that extends beyond the dance floor into the intricacies of their relationship."*
>
> *~ James and D'Leene DeBoer*

Step 3 - Connection: Creating Together

Connection is the lifeblood of any relationship, the vital essence that nurtures love, intimacy, and growth. However, it wasn't until we experienced the profound depths of connection through dancing with our person that we truly understood its transformative power in a relationship. In the early days of our relationship, we intuitively understood that feeding our connection was the key to unlocking the full potential of our love. We made a conscious choice to surround ourselves with friends, family, and environments that aligned with our values, knowing that their support and positive influence would help us navigate the challenges we faced as a couple.

It was on the dance floor that we discovered the true magic of connection. When we dance, we tune into

...And So, We Dance

each other's energy and spirit in a way that no words can express, nor are they needed. Our bodies speak a language of their own, expressing love, vulnerability, and a deep sense of belonging with every movement. In those moments, we are fully present, grounded in the here and now, united in a creative expression that is both beautiful and sacred.

Connection is part of why we love West Coast Swing so much. The connection to the music and especially to your partner through the stretch and compression feels amazing. Part of why it feels so amazing is it takes time and practice to develop while growing your appreciation for it the same as we do in our partnership. You also experience the different connections through music and dance partners the same as with different dialects of a language. Only the difference is our languages can create together with complete understanding and acceptance through the differences. This also works in our relationship by allowing us to be different while being seen, heard, and understood, which is what great connection allows.

Step 3 - Connection: Creating Together

As we've grown together, both as dancers and as partners, we've learned the importance of nurturing our connection in every aspect of our lives. We speak each other's love languages; expressing our affection and appreciation through dance has been a center point of this. We've cultivated a deep intimacy that allows us to see each other fully, with empathy and compassion, even in our most vulnerable moments. Connection isn't just about our relationship with each other. It's also about our connection to ourselves, to our own hearts and souls. Through dance, we've learned to tune into our own energy, to be honest and authentic with ourselves, and to embrace our own unique spirituality. This inner connection has been the foundation upon which our partnership has flourished, allowing us to show up fully and lovingly for each other every day.

Looking back on our journey, we can see how the threads of connection have woven themselves through every aspect of our lives. From the friends and family who have supported us, to the values that guide us, to the love languages we speak, to the energy we share on the dance floor, connection has been the constant that has held us together through every challenge and every triumph. Our movement together says everything words often fail to say.

...And So, We Dance

And so, to every couple who yearns for a love that is deep, passionate, and unshakeable, we say this: nurture your unique connection. Surround yourselves with love and support, tune into each other's energy and spirit, speak each other's love languages, and find a practice that allows you to express yourselves creatively and authentically. Whether it's dance or something else entirely, make connection the lifeblood of your love, and watch as your relationship blossoms into something truly extraordinary. Of course, we are partial to dance being the way and want to have you experience this magical connection with your person too. However, there are people who don't feel it when they dance and that is okay. Find something that is creative and non-verbal to share with your partner regularly. The simplicity of meditating together shouldn't be underestimated either and anyone can take a 10min meditation break with their partner to gain alignment, shift energy, or refocus on goals together. These things don't need to be complicated to connect on a deep level.

Touch each other! Physically, spiritually, emotionally, and mentally. None of these are verbal

Step 3 - Connection: Creating Together

and all of these connections are pivotal in having a deeply loving intimate and passionate relationship. So, touch each other as much as you both like to strengthen your connection, deepen your intimacy, ignite your passion, and see each other fully.

...And So, We Dance

> *"Dance is the non-verbal embodiment of communication, connection, and intimacy; it allows couples to go to depths with each other they didn't know existed."*
>
> *~ James and D'Leene DeBoer*

Step 4 - Communication: The Dance of Life

Communication, to us, is the dance of two hearts, a delicate and intricate choreography of words, gestures, and unspoken understanding. It wasn't until we stepped onto the dance floor together that we truly grasped the depths of what it means to communicate with each other's soul. Dance is a space where we can melt into one another and just BE. Anything that seemed like a struggle before no longer mattered because we were one and everything makes sense, without words, in this space.

In the beginning, our communication was clumsy, a tangle of missteps and misunderstandings. We have different communication styles and thought

...And So, We Dance

processes, so we stumbled over each other's feet, both literally and figuratively, struggling to find our rhythm in the dance of life. As we continued to move together, letting the music guide us, we began to discover the subtle language of our hearts. This doesn't mean we no longer stumble; it just means we stumble and recover together at a quicker rate as we learn and grow our skills.

Let the dance be an embodied practice of communication, a sacred space of presence and freedom. With each syncopated step, we learn to interpret the subtle physical, verbal, and energetic cues that allow us to flow in harmony. A gentle touch, a whispered word, a shared glance, these are the building blocks of our intimate communication, the foundations of dance and partnering.

Speaking of communication we are on the opposite sides of communication styles, verbally. We are also on the opposite sides of how we process information and come to decisions. This gives us many opportunities every day, and we do mean every day, to learn and grow our skills, have patience, empathy,

Step 4 - Communication: The Dance of Life

and compassion for our partner. We know firsthand the struggles of a partnership in communication when your partner is seemingly speaking a whole other language. This is another reason dance is so powerful as a tool to regain alignment and get out of your own way.

When you watch dancers perform a choreographed routine and it is flawless, they didn't get there without conflict or challenges. It is in how they faced those challenges and came together to empower the partnership and their end goals to create a masterpiece. They prioritize the partnership and getting to their goal, doing what it takes for them to come together and get there, because only they can create that goal together. Marriage and committed partnerships are no exception. We can just get lost in the weeds, losing track of the end goals and how we can come together to get there.

As we've grown together, both as dancers and as partners, we've learned to express our intimate styles vulnerably and gracefully. We've discovered the gifts in each other's communication, the unique ways in

...And So, We Dance

which we share our hearts and souls. And we've learned to recognize that perceived missteps are not failures, but creative variations/opportunities to enhance trust and attunement, to deepen our connection and understanding of each other.

Through dance, we've found a freedom in our communication that we never knew was possible. We move together without fear or hesitation, fully engaging in the dance of life, expressing our love and devotion with every step. Our communication has become a work of art, a passionate expression of our shared journey. It hasn't been without challenges, and we remember where we want to go as a team and decide how we are going to handle it together.

Communication isn't just about the words we speak or the movements we make. It's about the energy we bring to each interaction, the intention behind every gesture. In our dance, we've learned to ground ourselves in presence and connection, to let our hearts lead the way. We've discovered that when we communicate from a place of love and

Step 4 - Communication: The Dance of Life

understanding, even the most difficult conversations become opportunities for growth and healing. This deepens our bond and intimacy making our relationship that much richer.

Looking back on our journey, we can see how the dance has transformed our communication, both on and off the dance floor. We've learned to express ourselves with grace and authenticity, to honor each other's unique styles and gifts, and to find beauty in every creative variation. Our communication through dance has become a sacred language, a way of sharing our hearts and souls with each other every day.

To every couple who desires communication that is a safe, empowering, and loving space, we say this: let your communication be a dance. Move together with presence and freedom, express yourselves vulnerably and gracefully, and recognize that every misstep is a creative variation to an opportunity for growth. When you fully engage in the dance of life together, your relationship becomes a work of art, a passionate expression of your love and devotion.

...And So, We Dance

In the end, communication is the heartbeat of any relationship, the sacred dance that keeps love alive. So, take your partner's hand, step into the kitchen, and let your heart lead the way. With every syncopated step, you'll discover the uncharted depths of what it means to truly communicate with the others soul in the dance of life together.

Step 4 - Communication: The Dance of Life

...And So, We Dance

> *"We don't get to choose the music life plays for us, but we get to choose who we dance with to it."*
>
> *~ James and D'Leene DeBoer*

Let's Dance!

Dance is an art of redirecting energy... I remember a time we had a fight as a couple. It was one of those days where we were just off time, missing each other, nothing seemed to be working, it was a rough day with so much to do adding to the stress and pressure. It was a whirlwind of emotions, hurt feelings and misunderstandings that put us to the test. We were lost in our own pain, unable to see a way forward, until James took my hand and led me to the kitchen. He put on a favorite song, pulled me close, and started to dance with me.

At first, I resisted, because I'm stubborn and was feeling hurt. I was also in my head about the whole day and everything we were facing. How could we dance when everything felt so broken? As we moved together, letting the music guide us, I felt something shift inside me. The anger and hurt began to melt away, replaced by a sense of connection and understanding. In that moment, it was just us and the music, a sacred space where we could rediscover the love that brought us together in the first place. It's complete surrender and presence with the person I love and choose to dance through this crazy life with.

As we've grown together, both as dancers and as partners, we've learned that dance is more than just a hobby or a passion. It's a powerful tool for redirecting the intention, energy, and combined focus in our partnership. When we dance, we're not just moving our bodies; we're shaking off the negative emotions and patterns that can hold us back, making space for something new and beautiful to emerge.

We think about the advice often given in couples counseling, to hold hands while you fight. It's a way of staying connected physically and emotionally, even amid conflict. Dance takes this idea to a whole new level. When we dance, we're not just holding hands; we're moving together as one, letting the rhythm of the music guide us back to a place of

Let's Dance!

harmony and understanding. Our hearts and souls are connected as we move through the dance and metaphorically the emotions, worries, stressors. We end up at a completely different place on the dance floor and emotionally together in a tangible way.

Of course, it's not always easy. There are times when the last thing we want to do is dance, when we're so caught up in our own pain and frustration that we can't see a way out. That's where the true power of dance lies. It's a way of getting out of our own way, of redirecting our energy towards something positive and productive that unites us and shifts us back toward our goals. We can literally "shake it off" (pun intended) and restart.

In those moments, while we are dancing together, it forces us to pause and remember the blessing of having this person as our partner. Having a person who chooses to be "in" with us every day. The beauty of having a person that chooses "in" with you is you have someone who fully sees you, is willing to get in the trenches with you, and wants the same goals as you. This is a time to pause, count your blessings, see each other in your highest good and redirect to productivity. You want the best for each other. Your success is your partner's success and you both win together.

Is this all easier said than done? Why yes, yes, it is. However, you can put literal signs up to remind you to get out of your own way and be in TEAM with your person. We have a sign in our kitchen that says, "In this kitchen, we dance." Everyone needs some outside support and encouraging reminders. No one is without the need for support. Be that for each other and surround yourselves with the support that serves your highest and greatest good. If it helps set a daily alarm that has reminders to acknowledge your partner, highlights your goals, gives you acknowledgement or encouragement, etc. Let technology support a more connected relationship and better life rather than take away from it.

We are not in this dance of life alone.

Let's Dance!

...And So, We Dance

> *"You dance love, and you dance joy, and you dance dreams."*
>
> *~ Gene Kelly*

The Next Dance

Are you ready to take your relationship to new heights and experience a level of passion, intimacy, and connection you never thought possible? Join us on an unforgettable journey of self-discovery and transformation through the power of dance and partner connection either through our online courses or our in-person couples retreats.

At our life-changing couples retreats, you'll have the opportunity to step away from the stresses and distractions of everyday life and fully immerse yourselves in the art of passionate partnership. Guided by us, you'll embark on a transformative experience that will rekindle the spark in your relationship and deepen your bond in ways you never imagined.

...And So, We Dance

Imagine yourself and your beloved, moving together in perfect harmony, letting the rhythm of the music guide you into a state of intense intimate connection and presence. As you navigate the intricate dance of life together, you'll learn to communicate with a new level of intimacy and vulnerability, forging a bond that extends far beyond the dance floor and our retreat.

Through a series of fun and meaningful workshops, hands-on exercises, and heartfelt discussions, you'll unlock the secrets to nurturing a relationship that is built on trust, cooperation, and a new level of understanding of each other's needs and desires. You'll discover the power of creative vulnerability, the beauty of authentic expression, and the powerful impact that dance can have on your emotional, physical, and spiritual connection.

This retreat isn't just about learning new skills; it's about rediscovering the magic that brought you together in the first place. In a supportive and nurturing environment, surrounded by like-minded couples, you'll have the opportunity to let go of the

The Next Dance

distractions and stresses that often encroach on your relationship, and simply bask in the joy of being fully present with your partner.

As you journey through this transformative experience, you'll be guided by our personal stories, insights, and the wisdom we've gained from years of exploring the art of passionate partnership through dance connection. We'll share our own struggles, triumphs, and the dance-inspired lessons that have helped us create a love story that stands the test of time.

Don't settle for a mediocre relationship when you can have an extraordinary one. Join us on this life-changing adventure and unlock the secrets to a love that is passionate, intimate, and unshakeable. Whether you're a seasoned dancer or have never set foot on a dance floor, our couple's retreats will empower you to embrace the art of dance partnership and create a love story that will inspire all those you encounter.

...And So, We Dance

The music is playing, and the dance floor awaits. Will you join hands and join us on this incredible journey? Reserve your spot today and embark on an experience that will transform your relationship forever. Go to www.coupleswhodance.com for more information, read testimonials, to sign up, or contact us. We also have free resources if you aren't ready to join just yet and you can find it all at our website. We are also on Facebook, Instagram, and other social media if you have a preference. We love to share videos, tips, and more so stay connected. We look forward to meeting you!

...And So, We Dance

> *"Slow dance with me in the kitchen, where the world disappears, and it's just you, me, the music, moving together in harmony."*
>
> *~ James and D'Leene DeBoer*

In This Kitchen, We Dance

What dancing in the kitchen can mean for your marriage…

Life can be hard, busy, and draining. This can leave our marriage feeling disconnected and entangled in the mundane, where routines overshadow the spark that once ignited our passion.

Just a simple dance in the kitchen can allow you to increase your:

- Intimacy: It signifies a private and intimate space where you and your partner can express yourselves freely, fostering a deeper emotional connection.

- Playfulness: The act of dancing in a non-traditional setting like the kitchen injects an element of playfulness, reminding couples not to take life too seriously.

- Shared Activities: Engaging in a shared activity strengthens the bond by creating shared memories and experiences, contributing to a sense of togetherness.

- Communication: It serves as a non-verbal form of communication, allowing partners to connect emotionally without the need for words, promoting understanding and closeness.

In This Kitchen, We Dance

Dancing in the kitchen is a heartfelt celebration of love, transforming mundane moments into a canvas for shared joy and laughter. Embracing this enchanting ritual not only nurtures the passion within your marriage but also whispers a melody of support, encouragement, and unwavering togetherness.

Let's take a deeper dive into how this all works so you have some background information for your own understanding.

We all know that life has a way of getting hectic and overwhelming at times. The daily grind of work, responsibilities, and routines can slowly chip away at the spark that once burned so brightly in your marriage. Before you know it, you find yourselves disconnected, going through the motions, with the passion and intimacy of your early years feeling like a distant memory. It doesn't have to be that way. You have the power to reignite that flame and restore the

...And So, We Dance

magic in your relationship, by embracing a simple yet profound act: dancing in the kitchen.

At first glance, it may seem like an odd concept, twirling and swaying among the pots, pans, and kitchen counters. And for us, it has become a heartfelt ritual, a celebration of love that transforms the ordinary into the extraordinary. Because when you dance with your partner, even in the most mundane of settings, you unlock a world of intimacy, playfulness, and connection. There is something undeniably intimate about dancing in the kitchen, a private and sacred space where you can freely express yourselves without inhibition. We already create meals in this space which is an act of love in and of itself. As you move together, bodies intertwined, the world fades away, and all that remains is the two of you, lost in the rhythm of your love. It's a moment to bare your souls, to let down your guards, and to connect on a level that is beyond the physical realm.

This sweet dance is not just about intimacy; it's also a playful rebellion against the seriousness that often

In This Kitchen, We Dance

weighs us down. When you let go and dance around the kitchen, laughing and spinning like lovesick fools, you're reminding each other not to take life too seriously. You're embracing the joy and childlike wonder that drew you together in the first place, allowing your inner spirits to soar.

More than anything, dancing in the kitchen is a shared activity, a co-creation of love and laughter that strengthens the bond between you. Every step, every dip, every stumble, every breathless giggle becomes a cherished memory, woven into the tapestry of your life together. It's a reminder that you are partners, teammates, united in the dance of life, navigating its twists and turns hand in hand. Perhaps most profoundly, this dance serves as a powerful form of nonverbal communication. In those moments when words fail, when the struggles of life leave you feeling disconnected, the act of moving together speaks volumes for which there are no words. It's a language of the heart, a symphony of love and understanding that breaks the barriers of speech, promoting a deeper sense of closeness and empathy.

...And So, We Dance

So, the next time life feels overwhelming, the pressures of the world threatening to extinguish the flame of your love, turn on some music and invite your partner to dance in the kitchen. Let the melodic notes wash over you, guiding your movements, and allow yourselves to get lost in the magic of the moment. Because when you dance together, you're not just swaying to the beat, you're celebrating the incredible joy of being alive, of loving and being loved in return. You're breathing new life into your relationship, rekindling the passion that first brought you together, and weaving a tapestry of memories that will sustain you through whatever challenges life may bring.

In the end, dancing in the kitchen is more than just a whimsical act; it's a powerful ritual, a heartfelt reminder that even in the hectic or mundane, love can still flourish and thrive. So, take your partner's hand, turn up the music, and let the dance of life unfold in the most ordinary of places. It's in these simple moments that the extraordinary can come alive, and the flames of passion can burn brighter than ever before.

In This Kitchen, We Dance

Let's dance in the kitchen!

...And So, We Dance

> *"Knowledge is of no value unless you put it into practice."*
>
> *~ Anton Chekhov*

Practice, Not Perfection

Choreographing a lasting partnership just as partners intertwine in synchronized harmony on the dance floor, couples can use the foundational steps and connection of dance as a powerful metaphor for building a thriving, passionate relationship. This embodied practice provides a powerful framework for seamless cooperation, unwavering commitment, deep connection, and intuitive communication to reverberate through every aspect of life together.

When the music of life plays, who will you choose to dance with? In the dance of love and commitment, finding the right partner is only the first step. Crafting an enduring partnership that weathers the storms and crescendos of life with grace and passion requires mastering the steps of the dance itself. For

...And So, We Dance

us, that dance began quite literally on the ballroom floor. It was there that we discovered the powerful metaphor that partner dancing could provide for building a thriving, intimate relationship. The synchronized connection, the seamless communication, the ability to navigate challenges together as one unified front, these became the fundamental steps we applied to choreograph our partnership off the dance floor.

Over years of growth and facing life's tests side-by-side, we identified the four essential steps that have allowed our love to blossom into an enduring masterpiece:

Step 1 - Cooperation: The foundation where full responsibility, honest expression, consistent support, and aligning on your vision creates the fertile soil for intimacy to take root and flourish. Leading and following each other fluidly with grace and care.

Step 2 - Commitment: The driving force that propels you forward, wholeheartedly choosing this path together through the inevitable ups and downs. Honoring truths, uplifting strengths, moving through challenges patiently and lovingly as one.

Step 3 - Connection: The deepening bond created through vulnerability, belonging, surrounding yourselves with supportive communities, and practices like dance that unite your energies. Tuning into the spiritual frequency resonating between you.

Step 4 - Communication: The elegant dance where physical, verbal, and energetic cues are read with intuitive clarity. Flowing in harmony, using missteps as opportunities to fortify trust and attunement in your unbreakable partnership.

When these four steps are consciously integrated into your shared "dance of life", they create a powerful methodology for cultivating the lasting

...And So, We Dance

passion and profound intimacy that allows a partnership to withstand the test of time.

The dance metaphor also provides perspective, just as dancers must learn, practice, and hone their craft over years, so must couples continually nurture and strengthen their bond. There will be missteps/creative variations of the choreography. When that underlying bond is rooted in cooperation, commitment, connection, and communication, and two souls truly choose to "dance it out" together through whatever life brings, something beautiful is created. A living, breathing work of art that can only be co-created by the two of you, moving as one.

So, take your person's hand. Embrace your roles as partners, teammates, and soulmates. Let the rhythms of your hearts blend, and trust in the dance and in each other. When partners fully commit to the steps of this dance called life, they create a passionate legacy that will inspire all who bear witness to their extraordinary partnership.

Practice, Not Perfection

Let's dance, in the kitchen, through the rain, through the fire, the snow, and through this life together with our person.

> "Knowledge is power. Knowledge shared is power multiplied."
>
> ~ Robert Boyce

Resources

These are resources we have used or still use to this day and we're happy to share them with anyone. The coaches listed here we fully recommend and support. They did not ask us to promote them, and we asked them for permission to recommend them and share their information.

Obviously, we really want to work with you. we want to meet you and we want to know who you are, and maybe you're not feeling ready to work with us yet and that's okay. We're tremendous supporters of learning from different people and seeing what works well for you. The moment a teacher, coach, etc. tells you or leads you to believe no one knows better or can help you besides them. Well, that is the moment you know you're being gaslit for your money. We will add that you should finish the program you started before moving to the next, otherwise, you are leaving opportunities on the table. When someone creates a program, all the parts work together, so if you leave without completing all parts, then you won't get the full benefits. Don't do that to yourself and don't think a coach or program isn't right for you if you haven't done the work.

We consumed every free resource we could because we didn't have the money to invest in coaching. If you are struggling with finances, it's all the more reason to do this work and seek guidance with your struggles. Seeking coaching was the best decision and we wish we had known earlier in our lives because we could have saved precious time and struggle.

Please like and share, leave reviews so others have guidance when they want to know who's right for them. Reviews benefit everyone and it doesn't cost a thing. Much love and happy journey to you and please connect with us because we want to know what has been helpful to you! Dance in the kitchen, snap a photo and share using the hashtags #dancinginthekitchen #coupleswhodance

#andsowedance so we can celebrate all of the dancing in the kitchen fun with you!

Happy dancing!

Meditations and Mindfulness:

- 5 Minute Guided Morning Meditation for Positive Energy:
  https://youtu.be/j734gLbQFbU

- 10 Minute Morning Meditation - High Frequency Positive Energy to Start Your Day:
  https://youtu.be/QtRrDrf5uSQ

- Couples Who Dance:
  www.youtube.com/@coupleswhodance

- Forged Through The Fire:
  www.youtube.com/@ForgedThroughTheFire

- Growth Training Part One with Dave Scatchard: https://youtu.be/x9ixjdaJAh0

- Morning Meditation for Abundance and Gratitude | Mindful Movement: https://youtu.be/YejV-bnt608

- Positive Morning Affirmations (Self Love, Abundance, Gratitude, Joy): https://youtu.be/QudqAIVBVr8

- Positive Morning Affirmations for Success & Alignment Powerful Guided Meditation: https://youtu.be/tu1jk4li8YY

- Surpass Your Limits Mentor: www.youtube.com/@surpassyourlimitsmentor

- Sleep Hypnosis for Clearing Subconscious Negativity: https://youtu.be/_MCXtMjaJXw

- The Energy Queen: www.youtube.com/@sarahashleywheeler

Books:

- *Change Your Questions, Change Your Life* ~ Marilee G. Adams, PhD

- *The Universe Has Your Back* ~ Gabrielle Bernstein

- *Braving the Wilderness* ~ Brené Brown

- *Dare to Lead* ~ Brené Brown

- *I Hope I Screw This Up* ~ Kyle Cease

- *Gorilla Mindset* ~ Mike Cernovich

- *Atomic Habits* ~ James Clear

- *Good to Great* ~ Jim Collins

- *Forged Through The Fire* ~ D'Leene DeBoer

- *Can't Hurt Me* ~ David Goggins

- *Relentless* ~ Tim S. Grover

- *Crush Your Kryptonite* ~ Nate Hambrick

...And So, We Dance

- *Willpower Doesn't Work* ~ Benjamin Hardy
- *The Obstacle Is the Way* ~ Ryan Holiday
- *Girl, Wash Your Face* ~ Rachel Hollis
- *The Inner Critic* ~ Montriel Jamari, LMFT
- *Sis, Don't Settle* ~ Faith Jenkins
- *Don't Settle* ~ Molly King
- *The Anomaly Mind-Set* ~ Sandi Krakowski
- *The Attraction Distraction* ~ Sonia M. Miller
- *The 5 Second Rule* ~ Mel Robbins
- *The Four Agreements* ~ Don Miguel Ruiz
- *The Clarity Cleans* ~ Habib Sadeghi, DO
- *The Comeback* ~ Dave Scatchard

- *You Are a Badass* ~ Jen Sincero

- *The Untethered Soul* ~ Michael A. Singer

- *Leadership and Self-Deception* ~ The Arbinger Institute

- *The Body Keeps the Score* ~ Dr. Bessel A. van der Kolk

- *Extreme Ownership* ~ Jocko Willink and Leif Babin

- *Adult Children of Alcoholics* ~ Dr. Janet Geringer Woititz

Coaches:

- Jackie Bishofsky

  www.growwithjackieb.com

- Rebecca Blust

  www.freedomforlifeinc.com

- D'Leene DeBoer

  www.dleenedeboer.com

- James and D'Leene DeBoer of Couples Who Dance

  www.coupleswhodance.com

- Kim and Dan Graham

  https://linktr.ee/KGFinancial

- Montriel Jamari

  www.MontrielJamari.com

- Joshua Ludlam

  www.exponentialevolution.com

- Cheryl Lyons

  www.visiontoaction.org

Resources

- Sonia M. Miller

    www.surpassyourlimits.com

- Dave Skatchard

    www.allstarcoaching.com

- Monica Tanner

    www.monicatanner.com

- Kyle and Ariel Tresch of Couplepreneurs

    www.kyleandariel.com

- Sarah Ashley Wheeler

    www.tiktok.com/@theenergyqueen/live

- Amy Yamada

    www.amyyamada.com

...And So, We Dance

"...and so, we dance."

~ James and D'Leene DeBoer

COUPLES WHO DANCE

www.coupleswhodance.com

www.ingramcontent.com/pod-product-compliance
Lightning Source LLC
Chambersburg PA
CBHW032140040426
42449CB00005B/328